T0196407

MONEY PLANNING AND POSITIVITY

A GUIDE TO A BETTER FINANCIAL LIFE

JACQUELINE SCHADECK CFP®, AWMA®

authorHOUSE®

AuthorHouse™
1663 Liberty Drive
Bloomington, IN 47403
www.authorhouse.com
Phone: 833-262-8899

Published by AuthorHouse 11/18/2020

ISBN: 978-1-6655-0006-7 (sc)
ISBN: 978-1-6655-0168-2 (e)

Library of Congress Control Number: 2020918762

Print information available on the last page.

*Any people depicted in stock imagery provided by Getty Images are models,
and such images are being used for illustrative purposes only.
Certain stock imagery © Getty Images.*

This book is printed on acid-free paper.

*Because of the dynamic nature of the Internet, any web addresses or links contained in
this book may have changed since publication and may no longer be valid. The views
expressed in this work are solely those of the author and do not necessarily reflect the
views of the publisher, and the publisher hereby disclaims any responsibility for them.*

*This book is written purely for informational purposes. The views expressed are the solely
the author's and should not be taken as financial, expert, legal or authoritative advice.
The author has made sure all information contained in this book is accurate and verified. However,
the author does not assume any legal responsibility for any errors or inaccuracies in the book. Due
of the dynamic nature of the Internet, the links in this book may have been updated/changed.*

CONTENTS

FOREWORD

Wealth for many, seems like an aspirational concept that may be out of reach for the common person. It may also feel like it's confined to the concept of money, exclusively. The more life you live, the more you realize that wealth is measured in many forms, and in order to live a "rich" and fulfilling life you must understand how to create a diverse approach to being wealthy.

When most people hear the term diverse, especially from a financial perspective, they think about the stocks and bonds you have in your investment portfolio, after reading Money Planning and Positivity, you'll realize that there is so much more to being wealthy than the financial investments you have.

"The value of anything is the amount of life you're willing to trade for it."

I have been a financial advisor for nearly a decade, and it's been my experience that money is only fuel used to power your wealthy life.

In 2011, over 1 Billion drill bits were sold. What if I told you that of all of those drill bits sold, no one wanted the actual drill bit. Let's also assume that those drill bits were used to hang up beautiful artwork in offices and homes all over the world, would it surprise you that no one really wanted the art work either? What people really want is the feeling that they get, when they walk in the room where the picture is being hung.

Your money is very similar to this. It does not matter if you have a million dollars, it does not matter what type of account or fancy investment it is, all you care about is what you believe those financial resources will afford you the opportunity to do. Whether it's more time to spend with loved ones, traveling all over the world, helping others in need, the feeling of security, peace of mind etc. Ultimately, money just becomes the fuel you use to get where you want to go. So that's why it's so important to define what wealth means to you.

When you begin to explore what wealth means to you, it's important to think about what you value most. Then explore how you can create a life that aligns with your values in all aspects, not just financial. This book will give you the framework to explore what wealth truly means to you.

Money Planning and Positivity unpacks a practical and tactical approach to creating true wealth and abundance in your life. You will walk away with strategies you can implement immediately, to have a significant impact on your health, finances, freedom, social status and most importantly, mindset.

Jacqueline is one of the most well rounded wealth advisors I know, she created this book for you to use as a guiding light on your path to pursuing a wealthy life, I'm positive it will be a worthy tool in your arsenal.

Cheers to your wealthy journey,
George Acheampong Jr.

WHAT WEALTH MEANS TO ME

In a few short sentences, write what wealth
means to you now. You will complete this
exercise again once you've read this book.

_____

_____

_____

_____

_____

_____

_____

_____

_____

_____

_____

_____

_____

_____

_____

_____

_____

CHAPTER 1

WHAT ARE WE TALKING ABOUT HERE

"It's not how much money you make, but how much money you keep, how hard it works for you, and how many generations you keep it for."
— Robert Kiyosaki

In 1936, a 6-year-old boy in Nebraska began his first forays into business. He started by selling packs of chewing gum which brought him a profit of 2 cents per pack. He moved on to selling packs of Coca Cola, which made him a profit of 5 cents per pack. By age 11, he had saved enough money to buy his first company stock, and by age 14 he had saved up enough to acquire 40 acres of farm land. The boy moved from city to city and from job to job but never wavered from his core passion of investing. He took more courses, read more books and sought out a mentor. Like many people of his time, he survived the world war and multiple economic recessions. By 1969 he was worth $25 million and by 2008 he became the richest man in the world. The man I am writing about is Warren Buffet. Widely regarded as the greatest investor to ever live, and one of the biggest inspirations of my life.

While most of us may not be born with a natural affinity for business or investing like Mr. Buffet was, we can start with something, regardless of how small it is. And contrary to popular belief, you do not need to quit your day job or assume huge risks to become financially successful. As Psychologist Adam Grant argued, people who keep their day jobs while pursuing an investment or business idea are about 33% more likely to succeed than others who jump fully in. He argued that having some form of protection provided a psychological insurance for people, because it enabled them to take risks in one area of their lives, while keeping it safe in the other area. It is also so much better for our mental health to keep things a little cautious.

I was motivated to write this book because as a financial advisor, I've watched people make both poor financial decisions and great ones. Of course, we want to applaud the ones who make great financial decisions, but does that lead them to a great life?

Once I realized that great financial decisions don't always lead to a great life, I wanted to share why that happens and how you can do better. Yes, money can increase your quality of life, but it isn't the only important piece to a whole life. This book explores the four pillars to a better financial life and how they all work together. Overall personal wealth and what I've seen clients use to build a better financial life includes 4 types of wealth; physical wealth, financial wealth, social wealth and time wealth.

Working on these 4 pillars provides a firm foundation for anyone looking to get out of their financial ruts and achieve long-term personal success. It offers a holistic, vivid and practical approach to improving all areas of our lives, including how to begin investing, how to use your money to make more money, how to become mentally wealthy, and how to care less about what others think about you and more about what brings you happiness.

Imagine a future with less emotional struggles and less financial struggles. This book helps you to achieve that future.

Why should you care about Financial planning?

"Having money isn't everything, not having it is."
— Kanye West

Our society sends us conflicting messages about money. On the one hand we have celebrity culture and the literal idolization of wealth, and on the opposite side we hear statements like 'money can't buy you happiness'. The truth is more in the middle. While it is true that money does not buy happiness, it can certainly provide you and your family with the experiences to avoid being miserable. Moreover, poverty doesn't buy you happiness either. Quite the opposite in fact. A recent study by researchers from Harvard and the University College London found that rich people above 50 not only live longer than poor people, but are also like to have at least 9 more years of healthy living than poor people. Meaning, being poor could directly influence how long you live. It turns out having to constantly worry about emergencies, having no access to high quality healthcare, and the inability to purchase healthy food has a big impact on how long we live.

With almost 80% of Americans living paycheck to paycheck and 63% not being able to cover a $500 emergency, having a little extra money can go a long way in significantly reducing the burden on people's shoulders. It can also provide more personal and professional freedoms for people, because having money can make you less likely to stay on a job you don't like or in a relationship that brings you pain. Furthermore, money also provides us the opportunity to give the best of life to our families. It affords us the chance to give our kids a good education, and to go on adventures with our families from time to time.

Having said all these, money does not instantly solve all our problems. The world is filled with examples of wealthy celebrities dying from drug overdoses or suicide. It is crucial to know when to be content with what you have. Don't forget that good health, both physically and mentally, and our family/ friends, are more important than money. Money is merely the tool to get you where you want to go.

CHAPTER 2

PILLAR 1:
PHYSICAL WEALTH (HEALTH)

*"A wise man should consider that health is
the greatest of human blessings"*
— Hippocrates

The World Health Organization defines good health as "a state of complete physical, mental, and social well-being and not merely the absence of disease or infirmity." Having a good health has become so important that it is one of the highest priorities of the United Nations Sustainable Development Goals. It has also become a vital barometer to measure personal wealth. To quote Anne Wilson Schaef, "Good health is not something we can buy. However, it can be an extremely valuable savings account."

Having a good health is one of the most crucial things we need to pursue financial wealth, career success and to live a long, happy and fulfilling life. While being financially rich is vital for raising a family and for our material comfort, it should not be pursued at the expense of your physical and mental health. Many people spend their lives focusing solely on making money while forgetting their health and they end up with neither. Unless we begin to take our health with the same level of importance as getting a promotion or a raise, we will continue to watch many people experience hardships, which can lead to financial distress.

This book was written in 2020. In a period that will forever be remembered as the year COVID-19 devastated the world. In the United States, the virus has been responsible for taking more lives than any other flu or pandemic since 1918. The death totals have already exceeded the total number of US deaths from the Vietnam war, the Korean war, the Iraq and Afghanistan wars, and World War 1. This unfortunate reality has forced governments and policy makers to face how important good health is to the nation's economy and national security. It has also made families and individuals all around the world more conscious about the seriousness of having healthy habits leading to good health.

If good health isn't the best possible wealth, try imagining having a billion dollars but a bad health. Imagine constantly needing to visit the doctor every week. Imagine taking a lot of prescription drugs every day to survive. Imagine being in constant pain from the illness or disease you have and finding it difficult to sleep or eat properly even with millions of dollars in medical care. Such a person would probably be happy to trade everything in the world for a good health; for a chance to grow old and watch their grandkids play in the yard while reminiscing on the good old days with their kids. They would be willing to pay any amount of money to get their healthy years back and to be normal again. But as Reba McEntire reminded us, "All the money in the world can't buy you back good health".

Furthermore, if you need to worry about your health, it would be almost impossible to invest your time and efforts in other areas of your life. And if you always need to visit the doctor and buy medications, you would certainly have less money to spend on investing or pursuing your dreams. This is why developing a healthy lifestyle is the single cheapest and greatest investment you can make. It trumps any other financial investment because every other type of investment comes with some risks. For example, if you invest in stocks or real estate, the market could crash or your investment could reduce in value. However, investing in a healthy lifestyle has the highest guarantee of a good return for the rest of your life. It's been proven to guarantee less expenses on hospital bills and medications, and ensures a healthier, happier and longer life.

How to have a better Physical Health

The first principle of developing a healthy lifestyle is to note that tiny efforts over a long period of time are far more effective than those lofty new year resolutions we discontinue after a few weeks. Setting a target to take a walk every day is easier to accomplish than promising yourself you would lose 30 pounds. Leo Babauta says to "make it so easy you can't say no." Here are a few starting points to developing better physical health:

1. Drink more water

The research is clear. Water is by far the healthiest drink we can take because it is the purest form of hydration, and because our body is overwhelmingly composed of water, staying hydrated is an excellent way to become healthier. Water is also the cheapest drink available which means we don't have to spend exorbitantly to become healthier. Start by increasing your water intake by one glass per day and once you've mastered that, increase it from there.

2. Reduce your Sugar

Very few types of food can cause more long-lasting illnesses than sugary foods and drinks. They are bad for our dental health, bad for our wallets, bad for our weight and bad for our physical health. Deciding to cut back on your sugar would give you a big leap for living a longer and healthier life. By cutting back on one soda or saying no to one sugary snack a week you can begin to form a more health conscious mind.

3. Exercise regularly

Regular exercises are very important to having a healthier lifestyle. People complain about the price of gym subscriptions as reasons for not working out. But it is free to take a walk in the park. It is free to do a home workout, and to go on regular jogs around the neighborhood. It is almost impossible to live a healthier life without exercising regularly, so start small with a 5 minute walk everyday and build up your exercise regimen from there

4. Find your system of de-stressing

Continued stress can lead to many health problems, including heart diseases, ulcers, obesity, stroke, high blood pressure, depression, irritable bowel syndrome and migraines. This is why finding a way to unwind and relax from our daily pressures can be an excellent way to become healthier. We all relax in different ways, some of us de-stress by listening to music, some of us by watching movies or sports, or reading a good book, soaking in a hot tub, or playing a musical instrument, or having fun with your dog or cat. Whatever it is, you should find some time for it every day by starting with a five-minute dedication to your favorite way to de-stress.

5. Reduce your salt

Research proves that excessive salt can lead to high blood pressure, among other illnesses. In many instances, our foods do not actually need salt to be tasty. Moreover, you can spice up your food using natural ingredients, like lemon or lime juice, garlic, pepper and herbs. Natural herbs are a particularly good way to make our foods tastier, and they have been successfully used by human beings for hundreds of years, to great results.

6. Take the stairs

If you live or work in a building with several floors, it is so much better for your health to skip the elevators and use the stairs. This simple act is great for exercising your lungs, getting your blood pumping and working the muscles in your lower body. Committing to taking the stairs once a week is an easy way to start small and build your habits from there.

7. Sleep more

The role of sleeping in having a healthy lifestyle should not be overstated. A lack of sleep can increase the rate of having a heart attack or stroke regardless of a person's age, weight or exercise habits. Getting 7 to 8 hours of sleep every day allows our bodies to restore itself. It allows our cells to repair themselves, and gives our brains the chance to reboot. If you struggle to get adequate sleep every night, start building better sleeping habits by committing to an extra 30minutes of sleep every night and increase it as time progresses. Don't underestimate the power of putting your phone in another room or on silent to help you get to sleep faster and stay asleep longer.

8. Eat better food

We are what we eat. Swapping fast foods for fruits and vegetables is an excellent way to become healthier. Fruits and vegetables contain the necessary vitamins and minerals our body needs to function properly. Start building this healthy habit by eating one extra serving of a fruit you like per week.

THE IMPORTANCE OF MENTAL HEALTH TO OUR LIVES

"What mental health needs is more sunlight, more candor, and more unashamed conversation."
— Glenn Close

Believe it or not, depression is the leading cause of disability in the world and millions of people are affected by mental health issues every year. In the US alone, an astronomical 47.6

million people (19.1% of U.S. adults) experienced some form of mental illness in 2018, representing 1 in 5 adults. For serious mental health issues, the number was 11.4 million or 1 in 25 US adults. The situation is even more dire for young people from 18 to 25 with a 63% increase (from 2008 to 2017) in the number of individuals reporting symptoms consistent with major depression. The number of young adults with suicidal thoughts or other suicide-related outcomes have also increased by 47% from 2008 to 2017 (*All data are from publications by the American Psychological association*). These data points paint a picture of the daily emotional and psychological pressures that a lot of us face.

The U.S. Department of Health & Human Services define mental health as a person's emotional, social, and psychological well-being. Every year, depression and anxiety disorders cost the global economy about $1 trillion in lost productivity. As a part of our lifestyle, mental health is just as important as physical health. It is hard to say which one is more important, but sadly I've watched many people ignore the signs until it is almost too late. And because our society still struggles with understanding and accepting mental health issues, many people prefer to keep their problems to themselves, which can be detrimental. Furthermore, people with mental health issues are also very likely to experience problems in almost every other area of their lives. The National Alliance on Mental Illness estimate that:

- *People with depression have a 40% higher risk of developing cardiovascular and metabolic diseases than the general population. People with serious mental illness are nearly twice as likely to develop these conditions.*
- *19.3% of U.S. adults with mental illness also experienced a substance use disorder in 2018 (9.2 million individuals).*
- *The rate of unemployment is higher among U.S. adults who have mental illness (5.8%) compared to those who do not (3.6%).*
- *High school students with significant symptoms of depression are more than twice as likely to drop out compared to their peers.*

2.3 How to have a better mental health

If you face any mental, emotional or psychological issues, you need to know that you are not alone and that it is okay to talk to other people about it. Your emotions are fleeting and you are allowed to waiver in them. Extend yourself some grace during the low periods and work to determine what pulls you out of those low periods, so you can replicate the process when you're not feeling like yourself.

1. Sleep a lot

The importance of sleeping to our mental health cannot be overstated. Sleeping has been confirmed to help in regulating the chemicals in our brain that transmit information. These chemicals also play a huge role in managing our emotions and moods. To put it simply, one of the fastest ways to acquire a better mental health is to sleep more.

2. Keep in touch with your family and friends

There is nothing better for your mental wellbeing than having good relationships with the important people in our lives. Keeping in touch with our loved ones can provide us with the emotional support we need when we are at our lowest. It also gives us an opportunity to share the positive and negative experiences in our lives, and it can provide us with the validity needed to boost our self-esteem. With WhatsApp and other instant messaging apps, it is easier than ever to call and video-chat with our loved ones even if they are physically distant from us.

3. Volunteer or help others

Volunteering with a local school, a community group or a hospital is not just great for the people we help, it is fantastic for us. Experiencing the joy of helping other people is one of the fastest ways to boost our own self-worth. And being a part of a community doing some good in the world has a way of making us forget our own problems and feel better about the world around us.

4. Learn new skills or hobbies

Scientists have confirmed that learning new skills can improve our mental wellbeing because it can provide us with a new purpose and can build our self-confidence. Learning a new skill does not have to be boring or time consuming. You don't necessarily need to sign up for a software programming class to feel better about yourself. One could instead sign up for a cooking course, or a guitar lesson, or a dance class, or soccer practice, or yoga, or writing, or painting. Skills/hobbies like this also have the added benefit of being able to improve our performance at work. For example, a recent study of every Nobel prize winning scientist from 1901 to 2005 found that Scientists who were engaged in drawing and painting were 7 times more likely to have the creative breakthrough to win a Nobel prize. Writing plays, poems or short stories made you 12 times more likely to win the Nobel prize, and performing or dancing made you almost 22 times more likely to have the creative breakthrough to win a Nobel prize (*Study from a 2008 research published in the Journal of Psychology of Science and Technology*).

5. Do more exercises

I cannot stress enough how important physical activities and exercises are for maintaining good mental health. Research has irrefutably shown that exercise not only gives us a sense of achievement, but it boosts the chemicals in our brains responsible for putting us in a good mood. Even simple workouts, such as going for a walk, can help reduce mood disorders, anxieties, stress and tiredness. Exercise also helps our physical health and reduces the chances of having health problems. You do not need to become an Olympic long distance runner to exercise well. Walking, light jogs and stretching, when done consistently, can go a long way in improving our mental health.

6. Drink responsibly

Most people resort to drinking, smoking and drugs to improve their moods and feel better about themselves. But the effects are often temporary and we end up feeling worse the next day. Moreover, drinking for long periods can leave us with a thiamine deficiency. Thiamine is vital for our brain to function properly, and a deficiency can cause severe memory problems, confusion and eye problems. For smokers, being without cigarettes make our body and brain go into withdrawal, which can make us irascible. This is not forgetting the other health related problems associated with smoking.

And for other drugs, it is simply better to avoid them as much as possible. They can also cause withdrawal along with other unwanted side effects such as paranoia, low moods and anxiety.

7. Live in the moment

The power of being able to live in the moment is greatly underestimated. It can remarkably make our mental health so much better, including improving our feelings, our thoughts, and how we feel about ourselves. Rather than worrying about some hypothetical problems of the future, living in the moment can help you to appreciate the little things around you and it certainly allows us to better experience the joys of life. Wherever you are, be all there.

CHAPTER 3

PILLAR 2:
FINANCIAL WEALTH (MONEY)

"Do not save what is left after spending.
Spend what is left after saving"
— Warren Buffet

The earlier sections have fully explored the importance of having and maintaining our mental wealth as one of the pillars to a successful financial life. For Pillar 2, having a better financial life is about making the best financial decisions. Having wealth does not only mean having some extra thousand dollars sitting around for your next vacation, or even for something more serious, like a potential medical emergency. It is also not really about becoming a multi-millionaire. While all these may seem important, growing your wealth is about having something that will last you for a lifetime, and maybe for several generations. It is about building a financial foundation that will guarantee your financial security for life, including having enough wealth to live comfortably and happily through your retirement (or when you decide to stop working full-time), and possibly having something to leave for your children and for society.

The media's portrayal of financial success has been counter-productive to say the least. We hear more about the extremely rare lottery winners than about the millions of people taking the slow, yet steady steps towards financial wealth. We hear more about pop stars buying luxurious houses than we do about the many single Moms on Etsy and eBay, who have grown small businesses into consistent money machines. It is important you remember that for most of us, it requires extreme patience and discipline to grow real wealth. We must set long-term financial goals comprising our spending, savings, and investment opportunities.

Here are a few guaranteed steps to help you with growing your financial wealth.

1. Manage your spending

Spending less is not the sexiest path to becoming wealthier, yet it is an important part of successfully becoming financially free. This means that you are living below your means, or simply put, not spending more than you make. Reducing your expenses is one of the easiest ways to instantly put more cash in your pocket. It is very similar to getting a pay raise from your job, but you set the standards here.

To make it easier, write down all your major expenses and look for cheaper alternatives or maybe even cancel some expenses all together. Share your Netflix/Hulu subscription with 3 other friends and split the costs. Live in a cheaper apartment or neighborhood or find a roommate. Find cheaper, but still healthy restaurants or cook more. Use public transportation to save on your car expenses. Reduce your trips to the grocery store. It's almost impossible to eliminate all of your expenses, but the key is in managing them to the best of your ability and not spending more than you make.

2. Pay down high interest debt

According to the Federal Reserve, 41.2% of all households carry some sort of credit card debt. This not only tells us that people are living above their means and spending more than they make, but they are paying high interest rates as well. Many people will ignore the liability column on their Net Worth Statement and only focus only on building their assets. This is a common mistake especially if the interest you are paying out is more than the interest you are earning elsewhere. Even if it is more than the interest you are earning elsewhere, is it worth paying someone else to borrow that money?

3. Save

The importance of saving money, while generally acknowledged, is often ignored by a majority of people. Before you think about growing your wealth, you need to at least have some money set aside for emergencies. To put it differently, you can't grow the wealth you don't have. If an emergency arises how are you going to pay for it? I'd hate to see you have to rapid sell your investments at a low price because you need cash immediately. We absolutely need a savings plan before we can become financially wealthy. One of the easiest ways to save more money is to automate your savings. Perhaps you can automate them into your brokerage or investment accounts every month. This way, you grow your wealth without even thinking about it and it would enable you to spend what is left after saving, not the other way around.

After you have accumulated some savings over a period of time, you can begin to seek different investments to make this second pillar of financial wealth stronger for you.

4. Find a better paying job or negotiate a salary increase

Sometimes I have to play the bad guy and tell people that they simply need to find ways to earn more money. A sound way to do it is to ask for a raise at work. But before you go banging on your boss' door, you need to have an honest assessment of your skills, your performance and your value to the company. You can begin by searching online for the median pay in your industry or what rival firms are paying their employees with a similar job profile to you. Then go to your boss, and politely ask to receive a raise. Lead your conversation by proving to him exactly how much you have done for the firm and why you really deserve a raise.

The Bureau of Labor Statistics provides an excellent resource with a database of occupations that you can rank by median pay. Visit the Agency's website and when you click on individual professions, you can get detailed breakdowns of the median salaries of each profession and the associated salaries for different subsets of those professions.

After reviewing this information, if you still feel you are being undervalued and your boss refuses a wage increase, you should consider looking for another job or starting a side hustle.

5. Have a side hustle

If you have a hobby or talent, you should consider selling your services online ASAP. An extra $500-$1000 every month can change your life forever, especially if you can invest that money. What's more, it has never been easier to sell goods or services online. Websites like eBay, ETSY, Shopify, Upwork, Fiverr and even Amazon can provide you with an opportunity to reach customers in every part of the world. To make this more vivid, if you make an extra $5000 per year from an online shop or service, you would be $75k richer in 15 years. And if you make up to $20k per year form your side hustles, you would be $300k richer in 15 years. If you properly invest these extra income, you can expect to receive a return of between 7-15% over 15 years, making you even wealthier.

When I talk about side-hustles, I am not talking about doing something out of this world. I am talking about doing something you already love. From providing voiceovers and ghostwriting a blog, to selling customized T-Shirts and starting a drop-shipping business. Other ideas include selling used items on eBay, starting your own podcast or blog or YouTube channel, and providing product reviews online.

As long as you have a talent, someone somewhere would be willing to pay for it. Why not find those people?

Over a long period of time, and if you continue to control your expenses, side hustles can evolve into full-time work and even place you among the 1% of earners.

6. Use your money to make more money

One of the biggest differences between rich and poor people was brilliantly summed up by Robert Kiyosaki in the Rich Dad Poor Dad book: "The poor and the middle class work for money. The rich have money work for them." Using your money to make more money is the purpose of saving (beyond your emergency fund). We don't save money just to save money – we save money to invest it.

To become truly financially wealthy, you must find a way to delegate a task for every dollar in your possession. When you delegate those dollars to make you money you will begin to learn the power of compound interest. "**Compound interest** is the **eighth wonder of the world**. He who understands it, earns it. He who doesn't, pays it" is a notable quote by Albert Einstein speaking to the power of compound interest. Would you rather be the person who earns it or the person who pays is?

One of the best ways to allow compound interest to work in your favor is to invest in assets that do not require a high exchange of your physical time and effort for a return on your investment. Financial assets like stocks, bonds, mutual funds, ETFs and index funds are great for this. So is real estate, when done properly. To quote Warren Buffet again, "If you don't find a way to make money while you sleep, you will work until you die." I could not have said it any better.

Jacqueline Schadeck CFP®, AWMA®

FINANCIAL INVESTMENTS
YOU SHOULD CONSIDER

Here are a few financial investments you should consider to make your money work for you:

i. Invest in Stocks

Stocks are one of the most popular ways to truly build your wealth. They are an investment that means you own a fraction in the company that issued the stock. This entitles the stock owner to a proportion of the corporation's assets and profits. There are two major ways to profit off a stock investment:

a) **When the stock price increases:** You can then sell the stock for a profit if that is the investment strategy you choose, or you can hold on to your stock for a longer period with intentions to sell at some point in the future.

b) **As the stock pays out to stockholders:** Dividends are payments made to shareholders of a company from the company's revenue. They are usually paid out however, not all stocks pay dividends. Popular tech companies like Amazon, Facebook and Google are notorious for paying little to no dividends. They are referred to as 'Growth Stocks', which means the biggest reason for buying them is that you expect the stock to increase in

26

value, which would make selling them for a profit an option.

ii. Invest in Exchange Traded Funds, Index Funds and Mutual Funds

A mutual fund is often defined as a basket of stocks, bonds, or other assets. It's managed by an investment company for investors who don't otherwise have the time or resources to buy or manage a collection of individual securities themselves. Mutual funds have become so popular that according to the Investment Company Fact Book, the net purchases by households of mutual fund shares exceeded the purchase of corporate stock shares for the first time in 1954. And by the end of 2014, households held almost $12.5 trillion of mutual funds of different types (equity, bond, and balanced).

Index funds on the other hand are like a mutual fund that is constructed to match or track the components of a market index such as the S&P 500 or the Dow Jones Industrial Average. It became available to the public in 1974 and instantly became popular. Index funds are bought and redeemed directly from management companies and they do not trade on a market exchange. However, index fund's management fees are far lower than Mutual Fund's because of a lower need for expensive market research. While index funds are great for some investors, Exchange Traded Funds are far cheaper and easier to manage.

An Exchange Traded Fund or ETF is similar to an index fund because it also tracks an index. But unlike Index Funds, ETFs do not require active management and it can be bought or sold like common stock throughout the day. ETFs are sold on most market exchanges and provide more flexibility to the investor than a mutual or index fund.

iii. Invest in Real Estate

Investing in real estate involves buying, selling, owning, managing or renting out properties with the goal of making a profit. Investing in real estate can be an excellent idea whether you are looking to quit your 9-5 job or to save up for retirement or simply for additional sources of income. Real estate is a reliable generator of passive income, which can be received in the form of the rents paid on your properties.

Most investors pursue real estate because it is easier to understand than the stock market and because of the steady flow of cash that could be earned from rental income. It also does not always require your physical presence, making it an excellent strategy for side hustles. And they can also help to protect you against inflation because you can increase your rent as the inflation rate increases.

Finally, real estate properties tend to appreciate over time, making it an ideal long term investment strategy.

HOW TO MANAGE FINANCIAL INVESTMENTS

Online Resources

Before beginning your first financial investment, you need to do a lot of research about the investment strategies you intend to pursue, the companies or assets you want to purchase, and how long you want to keep the investment. The easiest path would be to consult a professional financial advisor. However, it does not hurt to do your own research. Here are some examples of some blogs, websites, magazines and newspapers providing lots of information for financial investors:

Yahoo! Finance - https://finance.yahoo.com/
Bloomberg - https://www.bloomberg.com/
Wall Street Journal - https://www.wsj.com/
Financial Times - https://www.ft.com/
Barron's - https://www.barrons.com/
The Motley Fool - https://www.fool.com/
Google Finance - https://www.google.com/finance
The U.S. Securities and Exchange Commission - https://www.sec.gov/edgar.shtml

Kitco - https://www.kitco.com/

XE (for currencies) - https://www.xe.com/

Marketwatch - https://www.marketwatch.com/

CNBC - https://www.cnbc.com/investing/

CNN Money - https://money.cnn.com/data/us_markets/

The Economist - https://www.economist.com/

Selecting a Brokerage Firm

Every trader or investor must create a brokerage account to be able to buy or sell financial assets, including stocks, options and ETFs. It has become easier than ever to set up a brokerage account online and there are many brokerage firms in the United States offering investors different types of accounts for some fee or commission, or for no upfront fees at all. Here are some of the leading online brokerage firms:

i. **JP Morgan Chase** - https://www.jpmorganchase.com/ requires $0 commission fee and a $0 minimum balance to set up a brokerage account. It is excellent for making any type of financial investment.

ii. **E*Trade** - https://us.etrade.com/home this is a popular trading platform that requires $0 commission fee and a $0 minimum account balance to set up a brokerage account with the firm.

iii. **Robinhood** - https://robinhood.com/us/en/ this is a leading brokerage firm that requires $0 fees, commissions and minimum account balance to set your brokerage account and begin buying or selling financial assets.

iv. **Fidelity Investments** - https://www.fidelity.com/ although they are most known for being the largest 401(k) provider, Fidelity also offers $0 account minimums to open a brokerage account.

v. **TD Ameritrade** - https://www.tdameritrade.com/home.page requires $0 commission, but a $6.5 fee for OTC stocks. Account minimum to open a brokerage account is $0.

vi. **Interactive brokers** - https://www.interactivebrokers.com/en/home.php requires $0 commission, but with a minimum $1 and maximum 0.5% of trade value. Volume discount are also provided and the minimum account balance is 0$.

CHAPTER 4

PILLAR 3:
SOCIAL WEALTH (STATUS)

"What the superior man seeks is in himself;
what the small man seeks is in others."
— *Confucius*

Humans are social animals. If the Coronavirus lockdowns taught us anything, it is that we need other people, and that the idea of social distancing is far more difficult than most people ever imagined. This is not forgetting the fact that we only had a physical social distance not a full social distance. Social media apps like TikTok, Instagram and Facebook experienced an unprecedented level of usage during the lockdown. So did messaging and call/video conferencing apps like Zoom, WhatsApp and Facebook Messenger. We didn't really distance ourselves from people, we simply found other ways to seek social approval and connection.

After attaining some level of financial wealth, it is natural to want to seek social wealth, to want people to think highly of you. People often do this by acquiring fancier items to tell the world they are of a higher status. Suddenly, we switch from wearing a Timex to window shopping for a Rolex. Buying a Ford or Chevy would no longer be sufficient, we would want to own a Mercedes or a Porsche. Restaurants? We'd suddenly decide to start dining at more expensive options, and next time we are at the club, it is no longer enough to just have fun, we instead buy out sections. We join country/golf clubs and fly business or first class and rent/buy housing in fancier neighborhoods. The list is endless.

Adopting a life like this can be very expensive and we call this, 'lifestyle inflation'. It simply means that as your income increases, so will your expenses. It's similar to Parkinson's Law which says that your work will inherently expand to fulfill the time allotted. Comparably, your expenses will increase to fulfill your income, and maybe even increase past your income if you're not cognizant of this. Have you noticed yourself doing this? It takes a lot of self-control to manage this pillar and that's why it's in this book – because you can't spend all the money that you make if you want to have a better financial life.

HOW TO HAVE BETTER
SOCIAL WEALTH

I. Define your needs

Always ask yourself if you actually really need something before you ever buy it. This serves as a gut check to avoid accumulating a lot of things we never use. To make this work you need to have a very honest mental conversation with yourself before you buy anything. The simple questions "why do I need this?", "would I still want to buy it in 10 months?" and "can I spend this money in a better way?" are helpful.

II. Create a budget

I like to call the budget your spending plan. Having a spending plan allows you to delegate a task for every dollar you earn. It helps to avoid impulsive behavior and to rationalize your purchases before you actually make them. Knowing what's available to spend can help you to manage the social pressures to spend money. A lot of us want to "keep up with the Jones's" but are you keeping up with their debt? The chances are that you aren't and you also don't want those debt problems.

III. Don't do/buy things to seek approval from others

The first step to achieving this is to become mentally strong enough to do only what feels right for you. I refer to this mental strength as being mentally wealthy. Building your mental wealth will help mitigate the need to look to others to feel good enough about your choices and decisions. While this does not mean you should not seek to have a connection or value with other people, it means you do not make financial or emotional decisions because of them. You do it solely for yourself. I want you to be mentally wealthy.

IV. Look for a free, cheaper or heavily discounted alternative

You don't always need to purchase the super-premium, luxury, newest edition of everything. The next time you decide to join a night out with friends or your local country club, know that you don't have to choose the most expensive option. If you are really going to buy that Mercedes, search until you find something that fits your budget – maybe that's the 4 year old model. Next time you decide to buy a Louis Vuitton or Gucci outfit, make sure it comes with a 70% discount which might place the price somewhere along your shopping budget, or simply say no to the purchase. If there's something that Coronavirus taught us, it's that you are capable of staying home and not spending money. As human beings we will continue to seek social value from others, not doing so at the expense of our financial, mental or physical wealth is imperative.

CHAPTER 5

PILLAR 4 - TIME WEALTH (FREEDOM)

"There is one kind of robber whom the law does not strike at, and who steals what is most precious to men: time."
— Napoleon Bonaparte

Time is one of the most important assets we have as human beings. Yes, it is an asset and we all know it's limited. And time wealth means having the freedom to do whatever you want, while being able to get the highest returns from your time. In the current fast-paced system of the world, time wealth is something that is not very often seen because people spend most of their lives working to earn money. There is a very popular quote about how the poor spend all their time trying to make money, while the rich spend their money to buy time.

A big fact about time is that all individuals have the same 24 hours every day, and what we do with those 24 hours can determine a lot about our current lives and our futures. However, having money gives you an opportunity to use your time as you see fit instead of completing tasks that need to be done as part of everyday life. Meaning, money gives us the opportunity to buy more time in a sense.

Take eating out as an example. When you order take out or eat in a restaurant, you spend more money than you would if you cook at home, but you save significantly more time which would have gone into thinking about what to buy, what to cook, the time for cooking, and cleaning process after cooking and eating. This precious time could be invested in doing something that brings you value, such as reading a book for your kids or learning a new course, or reading about a new investment strategy. It is a similar experience when you hire a Chef, a house cleaner, a gardener or a virtual assistant. The extra time you get from outsourcing these tasks can be spent on far more productive endeavours, giving you the freedom to maximize every hour of the day.

To become more time wealthy, we must learn how to manage our time more effectively. Here are a few ways to do that:

1. **Track your time:** The first step to managing time is to actually find out where and how you spend your usual 24 hours. For example, when you ask someone how much time they spend on their jobs, they mostly tell you

about the number of hours they spend at work, but they never consider the additional time it takes to commute to work and return home. Therefore, it is important to know what exactly fills up your 24 hours every day. And find ways to reduce the irrelevant things.

2. **Limit your time:** Setting time limits for finishing tasks can not only help us become more effective, it can also limit our distractions. When you know you've got a maximum of 30 minutes for a shower, you are likely to spend less of it thinking in the bathroom. Since many of us are now working from home, distractions can easily find their way into our lives. If you find yourself distracted, give into that distraction for a specified period of time, I like to use 7 minutes. Then refocus on your task and you'll be surprised how refreshing it can be. By putting a small effort in deciding how much time every activity/task needs, you gain a better grip of your schedule and are less likely to have different tasks overlapping with each other or going undone.

3. **Organize your time:** Utilize your calendar more effectively. Write down your meetings, deadlines, goals and tasks, among others. Plan and dedicate days to suit specific tasks. For example, you should plan a meeting about your company's cash flow only on a day when the company's CFO is available. Moreover, research has shown that we are at our optimal functioning capacities

in the mornings. Therefore, you should plan your most challenging tasks in the morning or in the first half of the day.

4. **Plan Ahead:** Plan your days ahead of time. This can be done by writing a to-do list at the end of the each working day, for the next working day. It not only gives a clear start to every day, but it also stops the time wasted on non-essential activities/tasks.

5. **Break between tasks:** Back to back meetings or jumping from one task to another sounds good, but is it really an effective use of time from human point of view? The truth is, it isn't. Without a break it is hard to stay focussed, and as humans, we need time to clear and refresh our minds before moving onto the next task or meeting. We can accomplish this in numerous ways. Some people take short walks between tasks, some do it by having a little snack/coffee break every few hours, and some like to talk to friends, colleagues or family.

6. **Delegating/Outsourcing:** Delegating and outsourcing are real time savers. In fact, it gives you the supernatural power to complete multiple tasks at once. Although it can be a little risky because when you outsource your task you are not in complete control of the final product, it can also increase your productivity many times over. This is one of the biggest benefits of building financial wealth. It can allow you to literally buy time. In general,

delegating or outsourcing lets you use your wealth to pay people to do things that you don't want to do or things that take up too much of your time. For example, if you spend 3 hours driving every day, you can instead hire a driver and spend your commuting hours reading a book, or working on something far more productive.

7. **Learn to say 'No':** Saying 'no' is one of the shortest words but it is also one of the hardest to say. If you already know you are exhausted, it is better to say no than to put excessive pressure on yourself. This can lead to additional stress and poor eating habits, which are bad for your physical and mental health. It is often hard to say 'no' especially to things about work and family. But if you have followed all the steps above, then you should have probably made plans and schedule for all the important things and people in your life, making it far easier to say no to the less important things.

8. **80/20 Rule:** This rule, also known as the Pareto principle, was named after economist Vilfredo Pareto. The 80/20 rule is often used in business, suggesting that 80% of the results comes from 20% of the efforts you put in. In sales, it is used for suggesting that 80% of sales comes from 20% of the customers. The same principle can be applied to time management and other areas of our lives. It simply means that most things in life are not evenly distributed. To apply this to time

management, you need to find the 20% of tasks that covers 80% of your productivity, and make these tasks the centrepieces of your day. This way, you easily find the least important tasks and eliminate them or reduce the time spent on them. You can easily start this with your to-do list every day.

9. **Do Less:** Yes, literally, do less. This can be attained by slowing down, being totally aware of what needs to be accomplished in a day and focusing only on the things that matter. Once you do this, every action becomes critical and as a result you create more value and reduce time wastage.

It is often said that "Time is Money". This does not necessarily mean physical cash and the goal is not just to have money. It is about the freedom time provides us to live our lives to the fullest. Time and adequate amounts of money can provide us with the freedom to do what we want, how we want it and when we want it. This is precisely why time is a form of wealth, and the 4th pillar of this book, because without time, none of the other pillars – financial wealth, social wealth and physical health – would even exist. Your time is precious, use it wisely.

CHAPTER 6

CHALLENGES YOU MAY ENCOUNTER ON YOUR JOURNEY

On your journey to a better financial life, you must be ready to face the many obstacles that are likely to come your way. The journey to becoming wealthier is a road less travelled by a lot of people. Therefore, you might face a few lonely moments when you begin moving along this route. You might find it very difficult to overcome addictions in order to become better. You might have difficulties cutting out unproductive friendships and relations. And you would definitely have bad days, in which you feel like everything is falling apart. All of this is totally normal. What counts is the effort required to become better. Growing your wealth is a marathon, not a sprint. So long as you are moving in the right direction, it does not matter how quickly or slowly you are moving. It is also never too late to get started.

Like it is said, every problem has a solution. While some challenges can get in the way of you achieving your financial freedom, there are ways to overcome them. But in order to overcome them, you need to understand the challenges that hold you back in the first place, so you can avoid them.

i. **Friends:** Some of the biggest problems you would face when trying to change your lifestyle would come from your friends. If you previously went to fast-foods together, they might not take your newfound veggie diets very well. If you used to go to expensive bars, they might make fun of your newfound habit of seeking a cheaper alternative. Knowing how to manage this change could determine your future.

ii. **Social/peer pressures:** If everyone at your job wears a Rolex, you might find it difficult to wear a Casio watch. Moreover, many people drink, smoke and use drugs due to influences from their peers. Peer pressure is the enemy of true financial freedom.

iii. **Lack of money:** Having the best financial advisors would not make much of a difference unless you have the money to invest. There are many people who would like to grow their investments but do not have the necessary cash to make this happen. Unless you inherited a sizable Trust Fund, you would likely face tough financial situations before you are able to grow your wealth. Don't let these stop you. You can achieve any realistic goal that you set.

iv. **Knowledge:** Many people simply do not know any way to become wealthier. If you took a random poll of people walking the street on a busy day, very few would be able to tell you the meaning of Exchange Traded Funds or mutual funds, among others. Of course, you're more knowledgeable after reading this book, but don't let this be the end of your journey. I implore you to continue learning.

v. **Poor health:** It is the most unpleasant situation that can happen to anyone, especially if the illness is a chronic or serious condition. Having a health emergency destroys any long term financial plans that a person can have and that's why it's the first pillar of this book. You would want to avoid becoming overwhelmed if this happens. You can manage this situation by having a good medical policy for you and your family, which could ensure that you do not get on the brink of financial ruin after a health emergency.

vi. **Losing your job:** Losing the job or primary household income is also another unpleasant situation that can happen to anyone especially during a recession or in the middle of a pandemic, such as the COVID-19. It is especially painful when people are laid off through no fault of their own, often times because of the financial condition of their companies or due to a market recession. Many families stop functioning normally when this happens. The best way to overcome this issue is to ensure that you and your family have an emergency savings with enough money to get you through a situation such as those listed above.

A FINAL NOTE

I'm so happy you've taken the time to read this book! Your dedication to reading this through to the end tells me that you have been searching for ways to create a better financial life for yourself. I hope this book has empowered and challenged you to become a better version of yourself.

Remember, we all fall off track or miss the mark sometimes, but that's no reason to give up. The foundation of your life's success will be built upon these four pillars and how well you can manage them. I wish you an excellent financial future. You can do this!

WHAT WEALTH MEANS TO ME

_____

_____

_____

_____

_____

_____

_____

_____

_____

_____

_____

_____

_____

_____

_____

_____

_____

_____

_____

_____

_____

_____

_____

Printed in the United States
By Bookmasters